4

Instant Pot for
Two Cookbook

Easy and Healthy Instant Pot
Recipes Cookbook for 2

Alice Newman

D1041598

Table of Contents

Introduction

Congratulations on downloading Instant Pot Recipes for Two: Easy, Healthy and Fast Meals for Your Pressure Cooker and thank you for doing so. New ways of cooking come along quite frequently, but for every hit, there are often a dozen or more misses that are destined to be sold during late night infomercials and nowhere else. With so much junk cluttering the market, it is easy to be skeptical, but rest assured, the Instant Pot cooker is likely the biggest thing to happen in cooking this decade.

The Instant Pot cooker is a multi-tasking device that serves as a browning pan, warming pot, slow cooker, steamer, sauté pan, electric cooker, rice cooker, and yogurt maker. Even better, it is capable of all these different things at just the touch of a few buttons and often cooks food faster than a more traditional alternative, all without using any gimmicks or microwave technology. Just like with most modern slow cookers, it also offers the ability to set a delayed programmable start time.

This does not mean that the device is not without a learning curve, however, as it is positively covered with buttons, many of which, on the surface, sound as if they have very similar functions. As such, this introduction will take you through the basics of using your Instant Pot to ensure you make the most of this extremely useful device.

What is Instant Pot

The basic Instant Pot comes with the unit itself, a lid, an interior pot, a plastic piece to collect condensation, a trivet and utensils. Assembling the unit is very intuitive, you plug in the power cord, place the interior pot into the Instant Pot, place the lid on top, and you are good to go. You will find the spot for the condensation collector to slide into place on the back of the Instant Pot, near the base. In general, you will not see much condensation collect back here; it is only for heavy flow scenarios.

The lid of the Instant Pot warrants a closer look as you will frequently be dealing with the steamer function which will, in turn, require caution as the steam will easily be hot enough to cause burns that may not be serious, but will certainly be painful. To lock the lid, you are going to move the steam release handle into the sealing position. The top of the lid also features a float valve that pushes up from inside of the lid. This valve will be down when the Instant Pot is not at a maximum pressure which serves as a visual indicator as to if it is safe to open or not.

Inside of the lid you will see where the float valve connects, along with the exhaust valve which is covered to keep it working properly. You will want to practice removing the covering of the exhaust valve before you use the Instant Pot to ensure you know what you are doing before it needs cleaning. Regular cleaning of the exhaust valve is key to ensuring your Instant Pot remains at peak functionality. Occasionally, you will also need to clean the float valve, to do so you will need to remove the silicone covering beforehand, it should come off easily as long as it is cleaned regularly.

The inside of the lid also features a sealing ring, which sits on a metal rack that can also be removed for cleaning purposes. It is important to be extremely careful with this sealing ring as if it is stretched or altered in any way, it will be impossible for the Instant Pot to generate a reliable seal, severely limiting its versatility. The lid can also be propped open by simply inserting one of the fins into the notch in the handle on the base of the Instant Pot.

To close the Instant Pot securely, all you need to do is to place the lid on the unit so the arrows on the cooker and the arrows on the lid line up. Turning the lid will then align the arrow on the lid to align with the closed lock picture on the base. This will require a clockwise movement and will be accompanied by a chime if the unit is plugged in. Opening the Instant Pot requires a counter-clockwise movement and will also be accompanied by a chime if the unit is plugged in.

Water test

If you have not yet used your Instant Pot to steam cook something, it is important that you first complete the water test to ensure the unit is not defective. This test will also serve to familiarize yourself somewhat with the controls.

For starters, you will want to make sure the inner pot is properly situated in the Instant Pot. With it properly seated you will want to add 3 cups of water to the inner pot. Close the Instant, Pot, taking care to listen for the chime, before pressing the steam button, followed by setting the unit for 2 minutes by pressing the minus button until the display reads 2.

If done correctly, the unit will shift to a display reading "on", up until the point cooking pressure is reached. Once this occurs, the float valve will engage, and the display will shift to show the amount of time remaining until the meal is ready. All told, this process will take about 5 minutes and may be accompanied by a noticeably plastic smell. If this occurs, complete the rest of the process and run through it a second time, the smell should not occur the second time.

Once the unit has finished cooking, you will hear a beep, and the Instant Pot will switch into standby mode which will keep your meal warm. If this mode is activated, you will see an L followed by an increasing timer that shows how long this mode has been engaged. This mode will remain active for 14 hours. To cancel this mode, you simply push the cancel button.

Remember, as long as the float valve is in place you won't be able to open the Instant Pot. To open it successfully you will either need to manually release the built-up steam, known as a quick release or wait for the float valve release on its own, known as a natural release. A natural release can take up to 30 minutes depending on the length of time the pressure was maintained.

To initiate a quick release, all you need to do is push the pressure release handle from the position marked sealing to the position marked venting. It is important to be cautious when making the switch as the steam will burn you if you aren't careful. You may want to place a towel over the vent to deflect the steam away from your face.

How to Use the Buttons

Keep Warm/Cancel Button

This button is pretty self-explanatory. You press this button to either cancel a cooking function or if you want to switch off your Instant Pot. You can also click on the Adjust button to increase and even reduce the heat of the Pot.

Sauté Button

This function is to sauté your ingredients in the pot, just as how you sauté things in a pot. You can also click the Adjust button and Sauté button for more charring and to a simmer, you press the Adjust and Sauté button twice.

Manual Button

This button has an all-purpose function. If your recipe mentions cooking on high-pressure for a specific cook time- use this button. You can adjust the cooking time with the '+' or '-indicators. There are also pre-set buttons that you can use instead of the manual one. Most pressure cooking recipes already come with instructions on how many hours and minutes you need to cook a meal for. But with the Instant Cooker Pot, it makes your life easier if in the event you do not have any available recipes or if you want to build or make something from scratch. The preset buttons guide you into determining the amount of time needed for an individual meal.

Here's a list of these buttons and what they can do for pressure cooking:

To make soup

For delicious soups, pressure-cook them on high for 30 minutes cook time. All you need to do is put all your ingredients in the pot, press the 'Soup' time and the 'Adjust' button once (more) increase cook time to forty minutes. If you want to cook for twenty minutes, press 'Soup' and 'Adjust' twice (less) to cook for less time. No more slaving over the stove to make the perfect soup.

For meat & stews

High-pressure cook time is required for 35 minutes for meats and stews, so the meat drops off the bone. To adjust more, click on Adjust more to cook for 45 minutes and to cook less, adjust less to cook for 20 minutes.

For Beans & Chili

30-minute cook time on high-pressure is required. To add more time, press 'Adjust' '+' to increase to 45 minutes and '-'to decrease to 25 minutes. The Instant Pot cuts the time in half when making chili.

For Poultry

You want the meat tender but not too flaky, so the cook time for this is 15 minutes of high pressure. Of course, you can adjust to a 30-minute cook time with '+' or 25-minute cook time with '-.'

For Rice

Rice needs to be fluffy. Too much water and it's lumpy and too little water will make your rice undercooked and dry. The rice function is the only fully automatic programming on the Instant Pot Cooker. The electronic programming adjusts cooking time depending on the ratio of water and rice that you put in the cooking pot.

For Multi-Grain

Ideal to be cooked on high pressure for 40 minutes cook time. If you need to soak them, and then adjust the timer to 45 minutes soaking and 60 minutes cook time.

For Porridge and Congee

The texture you are looking for is soft and somewhat lumpy. Cook on high pressure for 20 minutes. To add more tie, press Adjust '+' to cook for 30 minutes. For less adjust '-for 15 min cook time.

For Steaming

Use a steamer basket or a rack for this function because you want to prevent the food from having to touch the bottom of the pot when it heats at full power. You can cook on high pressure for just 10 minutes. Once the pot reaches the desired pressure, the steam button automatically regulates pressure. Use the '+' or '-buttons to adjust cook time or use the Pressure button to change the fixed timing for lower or higher temperature.

Apart from the buttons above, you also have on your Instant Pot Cooker:

The Instant Pot switch which is set to default to four-hour slow cooking time.

You can adjust the buttons to slow cook at 190 to 210-degree Fahrenheit for low pressure, 194 to 205-degree Fahrenheit to normal pressure and 199 to 210-degree Fahrenheit for high pressure. Again use, the "+" and "-" buttons to adjust the cooking time accordingly to your desired doneness.

The Pressure button which switches to low or high pressure.

The Yogurt button to make amazing homemade yogurt and can be set to low or high pressure.

The Timer button which is ideal for delayed cooking. Depending on what you are cooking, you need to select a cooking function first, and the make the necessary adjustments. Next, press the timer button and the adjust button to set more or less cook time with then "+" and "-" buttons.

Cleaning your Instant Pot

As with any electrical appliance; before you begin, unplug the unit. Gather some dish soap and vinegar, along with a small scrub brush and a microfiber cloth or cotton rag.

Step 1: Separate the interior pot from the separate lid. Wipe the outside of the housing unit to remove any tough stains and other debris. You can use a small brush to remove the crumbs.

Step 2: Use warm—soapy water to hand wash the lid. Be sure to follow the instruction manual's directions for the smaller parts.

Step 3: Remove the steam release handle by pulling gently to remove any of the leftover food particles.

Step 4: Never remove the steam valve, but remove the anti-block shield from under the lid to wipe the steam valve. Reattach the shield by hand.

Step 5: Remove and clean the float valve. Take the silicone ring off, which anchors the float valve, and clean both sections and reattach when they are fully dry. Always be sure the valve will easily move up and down.

Step 6: Remove the silicone sealing ring to inspect for damage and remove any unwanted aromas. You should replace it if you see any damage, making sure it is properly sealed before using it again.

Step 7: Thoroughly wash the steam rack and inner pot of the Instant Pot. You can place it in the dishwasher or wash it by hand.

Step 8: Renew the finish on the inner pot with vinegar. The vinegar will remove the discoloring in the pot. Don't use steel wool products because they will scratch the surface.

Step 9: Put the Instant Pot back together making sure everything is fully functional for your next cooking adventure.

Steam Cleaning: You can also choose to add two cups of white vinegar or water to the pot. Slice up some lemon rinds—toss them in—and run the 'steam' function for two minutes with the sealing ring in position. Allow the sealing ring to air-dry.

Notes: Never immerse the electronic components into water.

What to expect from the rest of this book

Now that you have a better grasp of just what your slow cooker is capable of, the following chapters are set to provide you with a wide variety of recipes that you can use to take full advantage of everything your Instant Pot cooker has to offer. You will find breakfast recipes, followed by recipes focused on chicken, beef, pork, sea food, vegetarian and vegan options. These recipes are portioned for two servings each and were selected to ensure they were as low in sodium and carbohydrates as possible. Remember, to determine the net carbs in a particular recipe all you need to do is to subtract the listed carbohydrates from the listed fiber.

There are plenty of books on this subject on the market, thanks again for choosing this one! Every effort was made to ensure it is full of as much useful information as possible; please enjoy!

Chapter 1
Breakfast Recipes

EGG MUFFINS

This recipe needs 30 minutes of preparation, 8 minutes of cooking time and will serve 2.

Nutrition Facts

Protein: 23.8 grams, Carbs: 4.7 grams
Fiber: .5 grams, Sugar: .2 grams
Fats: 20.5 grams, Calories: 308
Sodium: 100 mg

Ingredients

- Pepper (as desired)
- Bacon (2 slices)
- Green onion (.5 sliced)
- Cheddar cheese (2 T)
- Lemon seasoning (.25 tsp)
- Organic eggs (2)

Preparation

1. Place the steamer basket into the cooker pot and before adding 1.5 c water.
2. Add the eggs to a measuring bowl before adding the lemon seasoning and beating well.
3. Add the green onion, bacon and cheese to two muffin cups before adding half of the egg mixture to each and stir to combine.
4. Place the muffin cups into the steamer basket before covering and locking the lid in place.
5. Choose the high-pressure option and set the time for 8 minutes.

6. Wait a few minutes after the timer has gone off to allow the pressure to decrease before using the quick pressure release.
7. Remove the basket from the steamer and the muffins from the muffin cups and serve promptly for best results.

ROLLED OATS

This recipe needs 10 minutes of preparation, 10 minutes of cooking time and will serve 2.

Nutrition Facts

Protein: 23.8 grams, Carbs: 7.4 grams
Fiber: 5.2 grams, Sugar: 2.7 grams
Fats: 15.1 grams, Calories: 100

Ingredients

- Brown sugar (2 T)
- Vanilla extract (2 T)
- Espresso powder (1 tsp)
- Rolled organic oats (.5 c)
- Almond milk (.5 c)
- Water (1.25 c)

Preparation

1. Add the espresso powder, sugar, oats, water and milk together in the Instant Pot cooker pot and mix well.
2. Lock the lid and choose the high-pressure option before setting the time for 10 minutes.
3. After the timer goes off, turn off the Instant Pot and use the option to naturally release pressure for approximately 10 minutes.
4. Add in the vanilla extract and mix well.
5. Recover the pot and allow it to rest for 5 minutes while the oats thicken.

EGG AND HAM BREAKFAST CASSEROLE

This recipe needs 30 minutes of preparation, 3.5 hours of cooking time and will serve 2.

Nutrition Facts

Protein: 22.4 grams, Carbs: 22.3 grams
Fiber: 16.5 grams, Sugar: 10.7 grams
Fats: 31.5 grams, Calories: 350

Ingredients

- Cheddar cheese (.5 c shredded)
- Milk (.5 c)
- Organic eggs (5)
- Ham (.75 c chopped)
- Onion (.5 diced)
- Hash browns (4 oz. cubed)

Preparation

1. Spray the instant cooker pot with cooking spray.
2. Add in half of the hash browns to the sprayed pot before topping it with .25 of the cheese, ham and onion and repeating the layers as needed.
3. In a small bowl, combine the eggs, salt milk and pepper before adding the results to the cooker.
4. Place the pot into the Instant Pot cooker before selecting the cooking option for slow cooker and setting it to cook for about 3.5 hours.
5. Allow the pressure to release naturally when the timer goes off before serving hot.

INSTANT POT OATMEAL

This recipe needs 5 minutes of preparation, 8 minutes of cooking time and will serve 2.

Nutrition Facts

Protein: 23.8 grams, Carbs: 14.5 grams
Fiber: 9.5 grams, Sugar: 8.2 grams
Fats: 15.1 grams, Calories: 230

Ingredients

- Nutmeg (.25 tsp)
- Brown sugar (2 T)
- Flour (2 T)
- Cinnamon (1 tsp.)
- Rolled oats (.25 c)
- Unsalted butter (2 T melted)
- Maple syrup (.5 T)
- Water (.25 c)
- Raspberries (3 T)

Preparation

1. Add the berries to Instant Pot cooker pot before topping with nutmeg and cinnamon and adding in the maple syrup and water.

2. Combine the brown sugar, flour, unsalted butter and oats in a small mixing bowl and mix well.

3. Add the oatmeal to the Instant Pot cooker pot one spoonful at a time

4. Place the Instant Pot cooker pot into the Instant Pot cooker and seal the lid. Choose the high-pressure option and set the time for 8 minutes.

5. Once the timer goes off, select the natural pressure release option and allow the pot to sit until the oatmeal thickens.

6. Serve warm for best results.

LOW CARB BREAD PUDDING

This recipe needs 30 minutes of preparation, 15 minutes of cooking time and will serve 2.

Nutrition Facts

Protein: 60.4 grams, Carbs: 20.4 grams
Fiber: 20.7 grams, Sugar: 3.5 grams
Fats: 3.5 grams, Calories: 300

Ingredients

- Egg yolk (1)
- Maple syrup (1 T)
- Organic vanilla extract (.25 T)
- Egg (1)
- Coconut milk (.5 c)
- Grain free bread (4 slices)

Preparation

1. Line a pot that will fit inside the Instant Pot cooker pot, using parchment paper.
2. Add the vanilla, syrup, yolk, egg and milk into a blender and blend for 10 seconds before adding in the melted unsalted butter.
3. Add water to the Instant Pot cooker pot before adding in a trivet and placing the line pot on top of it before adding in the bread to the pot on top of the trivet.
4. Add the results from the blender to the top pot, taking care to press on the bread to distribute the mixture evenly.
5. Place a small parchment square over the pudding.
6. Place the Instant Pot cooker pot into the Instant Pot cooker and seal the lid. Choose the steam option and set the time for 15 minutes.

7. Once the timer goes off, select the natural pressure release option and allow the pot to sit for 20 minutes.

8. Allow the Instant Pot cooker to cool for 5 minutes before using the parchment paper to remove the pudding.

9. Transfer the pudding to a serving dish and flip prior to serving.

BREAKFAST CHICKEN CONGEE

This recipe needs 50 minutes of preparation, 20 minutes of cooking time and will serve 2.

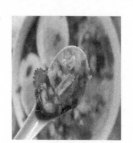

Nutrition Facts

Protein: 8.1 grams, Carbs: .5 grams
Fiber: .2 grams, Sugar: .1 grams
Fats: 14.2 grams, Calories: 210
Sodium: 180 mg

Ingredients

- Water (3.5 c)
- Chicken thighs (1 lb.)
- Shiitake mushrooms (1.5 c)
- Ginger (.5 in)
- Garlic (1 clove)
- Jasmine rice (1 c uncooked)
- Sesame oil (.5 T toasted)
- Soy sauce (.5 T)
- Peanuts (4 T)
- Cilantro (.25 c)
- Green onion (.5 sliced) – 1 Boiled Egg

Preparation

1. Crush garlic cloves, peel and slice ginger, slice the mushrooms into thin strips
2. Clean and remove skin from the chicken
3. Layer pot by placing rice at the bottom and then the crushed garlic sliced ginger and sliced mushrooms. Place chicken right at the top.
4. Pour in the seven cups of water

5. Lock and seal the lid.

6. Press 'Porridge' to begin cooking. No need to adjust time.

7. Once the cooker reaches the desired temperature and pressure, it will countdown 20 minutes.

8. The pot will beep after 20 minutes and turn to 'keep warm' setting, and the pressure will drop gradually. Allow pressure to release naturally without opening steam valve.

9. Once the float valve falls back to the down position, open the steam valve and then the lid.

10. Remove chicken pieces and place them on cutting board. Use forks to remove the meat off the bones and then shred finely. Place shredded meat back into the pot.

11. Stir porridge to combine all ingredients and add salt as needed, to amplify flavors.

12. Serve congee with a drizzle of healthy dose of sesame oil and soy sauce. Sprinkle green onions, cilantro and chopped peanuts to serve.

EGG BAKE

This recipe needs 5 minutes of preparation, 5 minutes of cooking time and will serve 2.

Nutrition Facts

Protein: 23.8 grams, Carbs: 11.8 grams
Fiber: 10.7 grams, Sugar: 8 grams
Fats: 11.2 grams, Calories: 182.7

Ingredients

- Cheddar cheese (2 T shredded)
- Spinach (1 c sliced)
- Eggs (3)
- Pepper (as desired)
- Hash browns (.5 c)
- Bacon (2 slices chopped, crisped)
- Milk (.25 c)

Preparation

1. Cook the bacon as desired until it is crispy.
2. Turn on the Instant Pot cook and set it sauté
3. Add in the hash browns and allow them to cook for 2 minutes before adding in the spinach.
4. In a mixing bowl, add in the cheese, milk and eggs and whisk well before adding in the pepper and adding the results to the Instant Pot cooker.
5. Close and seal the lid before setting the Instant Pot cooker to high pressure and the timer to 5 minutes.
6. Quick release the steam once the time goes off before loosening the edges of the egg and moving it to a serving dish.
7. Top with extra cheese prior to serving.

SCOTCH EGGS

This recipe needs 5 minutes of preparation, 5 minutes of cooking time and will serve 2.

Nutrition Facts

Protein: 23.8 grams, Carbs: 2.4 grams
Fiber: 1.7 grams, Sugar: 3.5 grams
Fats: 3.5 grams, Calories: 165

Ingredients

- Coconut oil (1 T)
- Ground sausage (.5 lb.)
- Organic eggs (2)
- Water (2 c divided)

Preparation

1. Set the steamer basket in the Instant Pot cooker before adding in the eggs and water.
2. Secure the Instant Pot cooker lid before setting the time for 6 minutes and the pressure to high.
3. When the timer goes off, choose the natural pressure release option before placing the basket of eggs into a large bowl of cold water to keep them from cooking further. Remove the shells when the eggs are cool to the touch.
4. Divide the sausage in half and use a spatula to flatten thoroughly. Wrap each sausage patty around an egg.
5. Turn the Instant Pot cooker to the sauté setting before adding in the oil. Once it is properly heated, add in the eggs and sausage and brown the sausage thoroughly.
6. Remove the eggs before adding the remaining cup of water to the Instant Pot cooker. Add in the pan insert and place the eggs on top.

7. Seal the Instant Pot and secure it before setting it to high pressure for 6 minutes.

8. Once the timer goes off, choose the quick pressure release option and serve hot.

LOW-CARB INSTANT POT MUFFINS

This recipe needs 5 minutes of preparation, 5 minutes of cooking time and will serve 2.

Nutrition Facts

Protein: 17.4 grams, Carbs: 15.4 grams
Fiber: 14 grams, Sugar: 3.7 grams
Fats: 12.4 grams, Calories: 157

Ingredients

- Egg (1)
- Baking soda (.25 tsp.)
- Water (1 c)
- Chocolate chips (.25 c)
- Zucchini (.5 c)
- Vanilla extract (1 T)
- Salt (1 pinch)
- Cinnamon (.25 tsp.)
- Unsalted butter (.5 T melted)
- Almond flour (.3 c)
- Cocoa powder (1.5 T)
- Coconut oil (.25 c)
- Can juice (.25 c)

Preparation

1. Combine the coconut oil, vanilla extract, sweetener and eggs together in a mixing bowl and whisk well.

2. In a second bowl, mix together the cocoa powder and the melted unsalted butter to form a smooth paste.

3. Mix together both bowls before adding in the flour, salt, baking soda and cinnamon and folding gently.

4. Add in the chocolate chips and zucchini and toss to combine. Do not stir!

5. Add the trivet to the Instant Pot cooker pot before adding in the water.

6. Add the muffin mix to a pair of large silicone muffin cups, a cookie scoop might help.

7. Place the cups into the Instant Pot cooker, separating them using parchment paper if there isn't room for them to sit side by side. Cover both muffin tins using parchment paper.

8. Place the Instant Pot cooker pot into the Instant Pot cooker and seal the lid. Choose the high-pressure option and set the time for 8 minutes.

9. Once the timer goes off, select the natural pressure release option and allow the pot to sit for 10 minutes before opening.

10. You will know the muffins are done if you can stick a toothpick into one and have it come back clean.

11. Let muffins cool prior to serving.

INSTANT POT HARDBOILED EGGS

This recipe needs 2 minutes of preparation, 10 minutes of cooking time and will serve 2. Cook a dozen at a time for a quick, and healthy, breakfast on the go

Nutrition Facts

Protein: 6 grams, Carbs: .6 grams
Fiber: 0 grams, Sugar:.5 grams
Fats: 5 grams, Calories: 78

Ingredients

- Eggs (1 dozen)

Preparation

1. Set the steamer basket in the Instant Pot cooker before adding in the eggs and water.

2. Secure the Instant Pot cooker lid before setting the time for 6 minutes and the pressure to high.

3. When the timer goes off, choose the natural pressure release option before placing the basket of eggs into a large bowl of cold water to keep them from cooking further. Remove the shells when the eggs are cool to the touch.

Chapter 2
Chicken Meals

SPICY CHICKEN

This recipe needs 5 minutes of preparation, 15 minutes of cooking time and will serve 2.

Nutrition Facts

Protein: 23.8 grams, Carbs: 18.9 grams
Fiber: 12.8 grams, Sugar: .2 grams
Fats: 22 grams, Calories: 223

Ingredients

- Black pepper (as desired)
- Jalapeno (1 diced, seeded)
- Paprika (as desired)
- Cumin (as desired)
- Onion seasoning (.3 tsp)
- Garlic powder (1 pinch)
- Chicken tenders (.5 lbs.)

Preparation

1. In a small bowl, combine the garlic powder, onion seasoning, cumin, paprika and black pepper and combine thoroughly. Coat the chicken thoroughly before placing it in the Instant Pot cooker pot and sealing the lid of the cooker. Choose the poultry high-pressure option and set the time for 15 minutes.

2. Once the timer goes off, select the instant pressure release option and remove the lid.

3. Let stand five minutes prior to serving.

CHEESY CHICKEN

This recipe needs 15 minutes of preparation, 25 minutes of cooking time and will serve 2.

Nutrition Facts

Protein: 30.7 grams, Carbs: 14.1 grams
Fiber: 8.7 grams, Sugar: 0 grams
Fats: 18.3 grams, Calories: 330

Ingredients

- Black pepper (as desired)
- Cream cheese (2 oz.)
- Cheddar cheese (2 oz.)
- Chicken breast (1 lb.)
- Bacon (2 slices)
- Water (1 c)
- Ranch seasoning (1 packet)
- Cornstarch (1.5 T)

Preparation

1. Turn the Instant Pot cooker to sauté before adding in the bacon and allowing it to cook until it is crisp enough to crumble.

2. Place the chicken in the Instant Pot cooker before topping it with the cream cheese and seasoning as desired.

3. Add 1 c water to the pot and seal the lid of the cooker. Choose the high-pressure option and set the time for 25 minutes.

4. Once the timer goes off, select the instant pressure release option and remove the lid before removing the chicken and shredding it with a pair of forks.

5. Turn the heat on the Instant Pot cooker to low before adding in the cornstarch and whisking well. Add in the cheese and then return the chicken to the pot along with the bacon and mix well.

6. Serve hot.

CHICKEN AND SHIRATAKI NOODLES

This recipe needs 15 minutes of preparation, 5 minutes of cooking time and will serve 2.

Nutrition Facts

Protein: 19.7grams, Carbs: 26.2 grams
Fiber: 21.5 grams, Sugar: 0 grams
Fats: 17.2 grams, Calories: 323

Ingredients

- Black pepper (as desired)
- Chicken breast (.5 lbs. grilled)
- Coconut milk (.5 c)
- Shirataki noodles (.5 c)
- Water (2 c)
- Cheddar cheese (4 oz.)

Preparation

1. Add the shirataki noodles and the water to the Instant Pot cooker pot and seal the lid of the cooker. Choose the high-pressure option and set the time for 5minutes.

2. Once the timer goes off, select the instant pressure release option and switch the heat to sauté.

3. Add in the cheese and coconut milk and stir until the cheese is melted.

4. Plate the grilled chicken and top with cheese shirataki noodles prior to serving.

TERIYAKI CHICKEN

This recipe needs 15 minutes of preparation, 15 minutes of cooking time and will serve 2.

Nutrition Facts

Protein: 15.7 grams, Carbs: 33.5 grams
Fiber: 32.8 grams, Sugar: 5.2 grams
Fats: 42 grams, Calories: 203

Ingredients

- Black pepper (as desired)
- Onion (.25 sliced)
- Water (.25 c)
- Cornstarch (1 T)
- Honey (.25 c)
- Garlic (1 clove crushed)
- Ginger (.3 tsp.)
- Low-sodium soy sauce (.25 c)
- Chicken breast (2)
- Rice vinegar (.25 c)

Preparation

1. Coat the Instant Pot cooker pot in cooking spray before adding in the chicken breast.
2. In a small bowl, combine the seasoning, garlic, onion, rice vinegar, soy sauce and honey and mix well. Use the results to coat the chicken.
3. Seal the Instant Pot cooker, choose the high-pressure option and set the time for 15 minutes.
4. Once the timer goes off, select the instant pressure release option and remove the lid. Remove the chicken before shredding it.

5. In a separate bowl, combine the cornstarch with the water and slowly incorporate it into the Instant Pot cooker. Turn the heat to sauté and whisk well. Let everything sauté for 60 seconds or the sauce begins to boil.

6. Turn off the pot and add back in the shredded chicken and allow it to warm.

7. Serve with shirataki rice.

CHICKEN THIGHS WITH TURMERIC AND CUMIN

This recipe needs 5 minutes of preparation, 15 minutes of cooking time and will serve 2.

Nutrition Facts

Protein: 23.8 grams, Carbs: 37.5 grams
Fiber: 32.8 grams, Sugar: 8.2 grams
Fats: 42 grams, Calories: 540

Ingredients

- Black pepper (as desired)
- Water (.5 c)
- Hot sauce (1 T)
- Black molasses (1 T)
- Honey (.25 c)
- Coconut oil (2 T)
- Lemon juice (.5 T)
- Turmeric (.5 tsp.)
- Ginger (.5 tsp.)
- Coriander (.5 tsp.)
- Cumin (.5 tsp.)
- Chicken thighs (1 lb.)

Preparation

1. Combine the spices in a small bowl and mix well. Use the results to coat the chicken thoroughly before placing it in the Instant Pot cooker pot along with the coconut oil and choose the sauté option, leaving the cooker uncovered. Brown the chicken thighs evenly.

2. Remove the chicken from the pot before adding in a little water, be prepared for it to boil quickly. Once the noise dies down, remove the brown bits from the bottom of the Instant Pot cooker pot before returning the chicken to the pot and setting the pressure to high and the time to 15 minutes.

3. While the chicken is cooking, combine the lemon, molasses and honey together in a small bowl.

4. Once the timer goes off, select the instant pressure release option and remove the lid.

5. Remove the chicken and cover it with foil to keep warm. Turn the Instant Pot cooker back to sauté before adding the honey mixture to the pot and letting everything boil, whisking regularly until the sauce thickens.

6. Dip each chicken thigh into the sauce prior to serving.

LEMON GARLIC CHICKEN

This recipe needs 15 minutes of preparation, 25 minutes of cooking time and will serve 2.

Nutrition Facts

Protein: 18.9 grams, Carbs: 22.9 grams
Fiber: 19 grams, Sugar: 11.2 grams
Fats: 28 grams, Calories: 453

Ingredients

- Chicken breast (1 lb.)
- Onion (1 diced)
- Butter (.5 T)
- Garlic (1 clove minced)
- Chicken broth (.25 c)
- Parsley (.5 tsp dried)
- Paprika (.25 tsp.)
- White wine (1 dash)
- Lemon (.5 juiced)
- Arrowroot flour (2 tsp)

Preparation

1. Set the Instant Pot to sauté. Put onion in with butter.
2. Cook for 5 to 10 minutes until onions have softened. If you want, you can let them brown.
3. Combine remaining ingredients, minus the flour, and cover.
4. Press poultry setting. The steam valve should be closed.
5. Let it cook completely, release the valve, and then take off the lid.

6. Now you can thicken up the sauce with a slurry. Mix a ¼ cup of sauce with the flour. Mix it in with the rest of the liquid in the pot.

7. Stir and serve. It will also reheat really well if there are any leftovers.

INSTANT POT FRIED CHICKEN

This recipe needs 15 minutes of preparation, 15 minutes of cooking time and will serve 2.

Nutrition Facts

Protein: 26 grams, Carbs: 32 grams
Fiber: 27 grams, Sugar: 4.2 grams
Fats: 33 grams, Calories: 477

Ingredients

- Chicken thighs (2)
- Coconut oil (6 c)
- Buttermilk (1 c)
- Paprika (1 tsp)
- Cayenne pepper (as desired)
- Almond flour (1 c)
- Cornstarch (1 T)
- Black pepper (as desired)
- Eggs (2 beaten with water)

Preparation

1. Mix together milk, salt, cayenne, and paprika in a bag with chicken. Marinate at least 30 minutes.
2. Mix in a shallow bowl flour, cornstarch, pepper and salt.
3. Pour egg mixture in another bowl.
4. Combine the rest of the salt, flour, and pepper.
5. Set to sauté and heat oil to 350 degrees.
6. Dredge chicken in cornstarch, egg, and then flour.
7. Ease chicken into oil with tongs.
8. Lock the lid and cook on high, 10 minutes. Turn off and release pressure. Carefully remove lid and chicken. Enjoy.

HONEY BOURBON CHICKEN

This recipe needs 15 minutes of preparation, 25 minutes of cooking time and will serve 2.

Nutrition Facts

Protein: 22 grams, Carbs: 26.4 grams
Fiber: 22.1 grams, Sugar: .8 grams
Fats: 22.4 grams, Calories: 367

Ingredients

- Chicken (.75 lbs.)
- Pepper (as desired)
- Onion (.25 c diced)
- Honey (.5 c)
- Soy sauce (.25 c)
- Ketchup (2 T)
- Coconut oil (1 T)
- Garlic (1 tsp minced)
- Red pepper flakes (as desired)
- Cornstarch (1 T)
- Water (1.5 tsp.)

Preparation

1. Put everything, minus the cornstarch and water, in the pot
2. Lock and seal lid.
3. Set to chicken for 15 minutes. For frozen chicken, add 10 more minutes. Carefully release pressure.
4. Take out chicken, and chop.
5. Set to sauté.
6. Mix together water and cornstarch.
7. Mix cornstarch and chicken into the liquid. Cook a couple of minutes until thickened.

Chapter 3
Beef Meals

SPICY KOREAN BEEF

This recipe needs 15 minutes of preparation, 45 minutes of cooking time and will serve 2.

Nutrition Facts

Protein: 23.8 grams, Carbs: 10 grams
Fiber: 8 grams, Sugar: 10 grams
Fats: 35 grams, Calories: 550
Sodium: 149 mg

Ingredients

- Orange (.5 juiced)
- Ginger (1 T grated)
- Garlic (2 cloves minced)
- Low-sodium soy sauce (1 dash for flavor)
- Beef broth (.75 c)
- Olive oil (2 T)
- Pepper (as desired)
- Apple (1 slice chopped, peeled)
- Bottom beef roast (1 lb. cubed)

Preparation

1. Season the roast as desired.
2. Heat the Instant Pot cooker to the sauté setting before coating the pan with the olive oil and allowing it to heat before adding in the roast and allowing it to brown.
3. De-glaze the pan using the broth, taking care to scrape up the browned bits before adding in the soy sauce and mixing well. Return the meat to the pan before topping with apple, ginger, garlic and orange juice before stirring lightly.

4. Place the Instant Pot cooker pot into the Instant Pot cooker and seal the lid. Choose the normal pressure option and set the time for 45 minutes.

5. Once the timer goes off, select the instant pressure release option and allow the meat to cool slightly before shredding.

6. Top meat with gravy prior to serving.

CHUCK ROAST

This recipe needs 25 minutes of preparation, 180 minutes of cooking time and will serve 2.

Nutrition Info

Protein39 grams, Carbs: 50.1 grams
Fiber: 44.8 grams, Sugar: 9.7 grams
Fats: 22.3 grams, Calories: 620

Ingredients

- Garlic powder (.25 tsp.)
- Unsalted butter (3 T melted)
- Vegetable oil (.25 t)
- Bay leaf (.5 dried)
- Low-sodium beef broth (14 oz.)
- Red wine (.5 c)
- Garlic powder (.5 tsp.)
- Onion (.25 sliced)
- Black pepper (as desired)
- Chuck roast (1 lb.)

Preparation

1. Combine the seasonings together in a small bowl and season the roast as desired, allow it to sit at room temperature for about 20 minutes.
2. Add the oil to the Instant Pot cooker pot and place it into the Instant Pot cooker before setting the heat to sauté and adding in the meat, allowing it to flame roast on all sides.
3. Add in the onions and allow them to cook for 5 minutes until they are soft and brown. Add in the red wine and allow it to simmer until it has reduced 50 percent. Make sure to scrape the bottom of the pan while allowing it to simmer.

4. Add in the bay leaf and beef broth before returning the roast back to the pot and sealing the lid. Choose the stew/meat option and set the time for 100 minutes.

5. Once the timer goes off, select the natural pressure release option and allow the pot to sit for 25 minutes before venting the excess pressure.

6. Remove the roast to the serving tray before running the resulting liquid through a strainer and using it to top meat prior to serving.

SPICY POT ROAST

This recipe needs 30 minutes of preparation, 90 minutes of cooking time and will serve 2.

Nutrition Facts

Protein: 35.7 grams, Carbs: 24 grams
Fiber: 19 grams, Sugar: 3.2 grams
Fats: 25 grams, Calories: 239
Sodium: 222 mg,

Ingredients

- Black pepper (as desired)
- Gravy mix (1 packet)
- Ranch dressing (1 packet)
- Pepperoncini juice (.5 pepperoncini)
- Pepperoncini (2)
- Unsalted butter (.25 sticks)
- Low-sodium beef broth (.25 c)
- Arm roast (1 lb.)

Preparation

1. Add the broth and pepperoncini juice to the slow cooker before adding in the roast and the packets of ranch and gravy, making sure to coat the roast thoroughly. Top with the butter and other pepperoncini

2. Seal the Instant Pot cooker, choose the high-pressure option and set the time for 90 minutes.

3. Once the timer goes off, select the natural pressure release option and remove the lid after 15 minutes.

BEEF AND SHIRATAKI NOODLES

This recipe needs 5 minutes of preparation, 15 minutes of cooking time and will serve 2.

Nurtrition Facts

Protein: 23.8 grams, Carbs: 21.9 grams
Fiber: 17.8 grams, Sugar: 12.2 grams
Fats: 28 grams, Calories: 394

Ingredients

- Black pepper (as desired)
- Yellow onion (.5)
- Mozzarella cheese (2 oz. shredded)
- Shirataki noodles (.5 c)
- Ground beef (.75 lbs.)
- Olive oil (2 T)
- Water (.5 c)

Preparation

1. Turn the Instant Pot cooker to sauté before adding in the olive oil. Once it is heated, add in the onion and allow it to cook for about 5 minutes until it is brown and soft. Add in the beef and brown it as well.

2. Add in the water and the shirataki noodles before turning the Instant Pot cooker to steam and letting the shirataki noodles cook for 5 minutes.

3. Once the timer goes off, and in the cheese and let it melt slightly prior to serving.

LOW-CARB MEATBALLS

This recipe needs 15 minutes of preparation, 8 minutes of cooking time and will serve 2.

Nutrition Info

Protein: 22 grams, Carbs: 19.2 grams
Fiber: 18.2 grams, Sugar: .2 grams
Fats: 18 grams, Calories: 223

Ingredients

- Black pepper (as desired)
- Mozzarella cheese (.25 c)
- Garlic (1 T minced)
- Parmesan cheese (.25 c grated)
- Ground beef (.5 lbs.)
- Olive oil (4 T)

Preparation

1. Combine all of the ingredients together in a mixing bowl before forming the results into 4 meatballs (2 per serving).
2. Turn the Instant Pot cooker to sauté before adding in the oil and allowing it to warm up fully.
3. Cook each meatball for approximately 2 minutes per side.

INSTANT POT STEAK

This recipe needs 15 minutes of preparation, 35 minutes of cooking time and will serve 2.

Nutrition Info

Protein: 25.6 grams, Carbs: 14.2 grams
Fiber: 12.1 grams, Sugar: 1.2 grams
Fats: 21 grams, Calories: 401

Ingredients

- Worcestershire sauce (1.5 tsp)
- Flank steak (1 lb.)
- ACV (2 T)
- Olive oil (.25 c)
- Onion soup mix (1 T)

Preparation

1. Set to sauté.
2. Brown the steak on both sides.
3. Add onion soup mix, olive oil, Worcestershire, and vinegar.
4. Lock and seal lid.
5. Set to meat/stew for 35 minutes. Carefully release pressure.

MAPLE BRISKET

This recipe needs 15 minutes of preparation, 40 minutes of cooking time and will serve 2.

Nutrition Facts

Protein: 23.8 grams, Carbs: 18.9 grams
Fiber: 12.8 grams, Sugar: .2 grams
Fats: 22 grams, Calories: 223

Ingredients

- Beef brisket (1 lb.)
- Maple sugar (1 T)
- Pepper (as desired)
- Onion powder (.5 tsp.)
- Paprika (.25 tsp.)
- Mustard powder (.5 tsp.)
- Beef broth (1 c)
- Liquid smoke (1.5 tsp.)
- Thyme sprigs (2)

Preparation

1. Mix dry spices together and coat brisket.
2. Set pot to sauté. Grease with oil and brown brisket. Lay brisket fat side up, and add thyme, broth, and liquid smoke.
3. Cook on high for 40 minutes. Once finished, let pressure release naturally. Remove and cover with foil.
4. Optional: Turn to sauté and reduce left over liquid.
5. Slice brisket and drizzle with liquid.

MEATLOAF

This recipe needs 10 minutes of preparation, 25 minutes of cooking time and will serve 2.

Nutrition Facts

Protein: 23.8 grams, Carbs: 10 grams
Fiber: 8 grams, Sugar: 10 grams
Fats: 35 grams, Calories: 550

Ingredients - Sauce

- Beef stock (2 c)
- Tomato sauce (.25 c)
- Tomato paste (.3 c)
- Basil (1 tsp.)
- Oregano (1 tsp.)

Ingredients – Meatloaf

- Bacon (6 strips cooked, minced)
- Onion (1 medium chopped)
- Fennel (1.5 tsp. ground)
- Garlic (6 cloves minced)
- Eggs (2 beaten)
- Oregano (1.5 tsp.)
- Ground beef (1 lb.)
- Almond meal (.75 c)
- Milk (.25 c)
- Cheese (.3 c)

Preparation

1. Mix the meat ingredients together.
2. Form into a loaf that fits in the pot.

3. Make a foil sling and put around loaf.

4. Mix the sauce ingredients in pot.

5. Put steamer rack in. Place meatloaf, in sling, on to rack. Lock lid. Cook on high 16 minutes. Turn off heat, and release pressure naturally.

6. Remove meatloaf. Hot pot to sauté. Simmer and reduce slightly. Baste over meatloaf, and serve.

BEEF STROGANOFF

This recipe needs 15 minutes of preparation, 20 minutes of cooking time and will serve 2.

Nutrition Facts

Protein: 60.4 grams, Carbs: 20.4 grams
Fiber: 20.7 grams, Sugar: 3.5 grams
Fats: 3.5 grams, Calories: 300

Ingredients

- Sirloin tip roast (1 lb.)
- Shirataki noodles (6 oz.)
- Olive oil (2 T)
- Almond flour (.3 c)
- Black pepper (as desired)
- Onion powder (.25 tsp)
- Thyme (.25 tsp.)
- Rosemary (.25 tsp.)
- Beef stock (.6 c)
- Paprika (1 pinch)
- Onion (.5 sliced)
- Garlic (1 clove minced)
- Red wine (2 T)
- Sour cream (2 oz.)

Preparation

1. Mix dry ingredients in bag. Add the beef and coat.
2. Set to sauté and heat 2 T oil. In batches, brown meat. Set to the side.
3. Add onions, cook until translucent. Mix in garlic.
4. Add in beef, wine, and stock.

5. Lock on lid, cook on high, 20 minutes. Release pressure.

6. Mix a little liquid at a time into sour cream until it has warmed. Mix into the meat mixture. Stir in pepper and salt. Serve over noodles.

Chapter 4
Pork Meals

PORK ROAST

This recipe needs 10 minutes of preparation, 3 hours of cooking time and will serve 2.

Nutrition Facts

Protein: 23.8 grams, Carbs: 13.2 grams
Fiber: 9 grams, Sugar: 2.2 grams
Fats: 3.5 grams, Calories: 360

Ingredients

- Coconut oil (1 T)
- Water (2 c)
- Portobello mushrooms (5 sliced thin)
- Garlic (2 cloves smashed)
- Onion (.5 chopped)
- Celery (1 rib)
- Pepper (.5 tsp.)
- Pork roast (1 lb.)

Preparation

1. Start by adding the garlic onion and celery to the Instant Pot cooker pot before adding in the water and then the roast, before seasoning as desired.

2. Place the Instant Pot cooker pot into the Instant Pot cooker and seal the lid. Choose the high-pressure option and set the time for 60 minutes.

3. Once the timer goes off, choose the instant pressure release option

4. Set the roast aside and place the vegetables and resulting broth into a blender and blend well.

5. Place the roast back in the Instant Pot cooker, seal the cooker and allow it to cook for 2 hours under high pressure,

this well help to render the fat and ensure the edges are crisp.

6. When the timer goes off, use the instant pressure release option and transfer the roast to a serving dish.

7. Turn the Instant Pot cooker to the sauté setting before adding in the coconut oil. Once it is heated, add in the mushrooms and allow them to cook for 5 minutes. Add in the gravy from the blender and let it reduce until desired thickness is achieved.

8. Top roast with gravy prior to serving.

BABY BACK RIBS

This recipe needs 30 minutes of preparation, 60 minutes of cooking time and will serve 2.

Nutrition Facts

Protein: 42 grams, Carbs: 2.4 grams
Fiber: 10 grams, Sugar: 6.2 grams
Fats: 18 grams, Calories: 450

Ingredients - Ribs

- Garlic powder (.3 tsp)
- Paprika (.25 tsp.)
- Baby back ribs (1 lb.)
- Chili powder (.5 tsp.)

Ingredients – BBQ Sauce

- Apple cider vinegar (.25 c)
- Cayenne pepper (.25 tsp.)
- Garlic (.5 clove minced)
- Tomato sauce (.25 c)
- Ghee (1 T)
- Black pepper (as desired)
- Paprika (.5 tsp.)
- Coconut oil (.25 c)
- Onion powder (.25 tsp)
- Bacon (1 slice)
- Apple juice (.25 c)
- Tomato paste (4 oz.)

Preparation

1. For the dry rub, combine the pepper, chili powder, garlic powder, paprika and onion powder in a mixing bowl and mix thoroughly.

2. Coat the ribs with the seasoning thoroughly before adding them to Instant Pot cooker pot which has been equipped with a cooking rack and enough water to cook the ribs effectively. Stack the ribs loosely as needed.

3. Place the Instant Pot cooker pot into the Instant Pot cooker and seal the lid. Choose the high-pressure option and set the time for 17 minutes.

4. Once the timer goes off, select the natural pressure release option and allow the pot to sit for 10 minutes before removing the lid

5. Remove the ribs from the pot and discard any juices. Turn the Instant Pot cooker to sauté before adding in the bacon and allowing it to cook until it is crisp enough to crumble.

6. Add in the onion and garlic and allow it to sauté for 5 minutes until the onions are soft and brown. Add in the remainder of the sauce ingredients and mix well. All the sauce to simmer and thicken for 10 minutes, sealed, under high pressure.

7. Us the instant pressure release when the timer goes off.

8. Top ribs with sauce prior to serving.

PORK CURRY

This recipe needs 10 minutes of preparation, 20 minutes of cooking time and will serve 2.

Nutrition Facts

Protein: 38 grams, Carbs: 29 grams
Fiber: 23 grams, Sugar: 3.5 grams
Fats: 33 grams, Calories: 520

Ingredients

- Carrots (2 sliced)
- Turmeric (.25 tsp.)
- Garam masala (1.5 T)
- Diced tomatoes (4 oz.)
- Zucchini (.25 diced)
- Ghee (1 T)
- Black pepper (1 pinch)
- Coconut milk (.5 c)
- Onion (.5 diced)
- Lime juice (.5 limes)
- Ginger (1 inch grated)
- Garlic (2 cloves minced)
- Pork (1 lb.)

Preparation

1. In a sealable container, place the meat before adding in the coconut milk, garlic, lime juice and ginger and mixing thoroughly. Allow the meat to marinate overnight for best results.

2. Place the onions, carrots, garam masala, ghee, tomatoes and meat together in the Instant Pot cooker pot and combine thoroughly.

3. Place the Instant Pot cooker pot into the Instant Pot cooker and seal the lid. Choose the high-pressure option and set the time for 20 minutes.

4. Once the timer goes off, select the natural pressure release option and allow the pot to sit for 10 minutes

5. After opening the lid, switch the Instant Pot cooker to sauté before adding in the zucchini and letting it simmer for 5 minutes.

6. Serve hot over shirataki rice.

CARNITAS

This recipe needs 20 minutes of preparation, 50 minutes of cooking time and will serve 2.

Nutrition Facts

Protein: 20 grams, Carbs: 12.2 grams
Fiber: 11.9 grams, Sugar: 11.2 grams
Fats: 7.5 grams, Calories: 320

Ingredients

- Bay leaves (1)
- Garlic (1 clove slivered)
- Oregano (.25 tsp)
- Garlic powder (.25 tsp)
- Adobo seasoning (.25 tsp.)
- Low-sodium vegetable broth (.25 c)
- Cumin (.5 tsp.)
- Roast (1 lb.)
- Chipotle pepper with adobo sauce (1)

Preparation

1. Set your Instant Pot cooker to sauté.
2. Season the pork as desired before adding it to the Instant Pot cooker and cooking each side for about 5 minutes. Remove the pork from the pot and set aside to cool.
3. With the help of a sharp knife, make a 1-in. incision in the pork that is deep enough to accept the garlic slivers.
4. Add additional seasonings to the pork as desired, rub the mixture into the meat.
5. Add the broth, bay leaf and the chipotle pepper to the Instant Pot before placing it in the Instant Pot cooker pot and sealing

the lid of the cooker. Choose the high-pressure option and set the time for 50 minutes.

6. Once the timer goes off, select the instant pressure release option and remove the lid. Remove the pork and shred using a pair of forks.

7. Return the pork to the Instant Pot cooker and allow it to soak up any remaining juices, taking care to remove bay before doing so.

CHERRY APPLE PORK

This recipe needs 5 minutes of preparation, 40 minutes of cooking time and will serve 2.

Nutrition Facts

Protein: 12 grams, Carbs: 22.9 grams
Fiber: 19 grams, Sugar: 11.2 grams
Fats: 28 grams, Calories: 453

Ingredients

- Apple (1 small, diced)
- Cherries (.3 c pitted)
- Onion (3 T diced)
- Celery (3 T diced)
- Apple juice (.25 c)
- Black pepper (as desired)
- Pork loin (.75 lb.)
- Water (.25 c)

Preparation

1. Add all of the ingredients to the Instant Pot cooker and mix thoroughly.
2. Seal the lid of the cooker, choose the poultry setting and set the time for 5 minutes.
3. Once the timer goes off, select the quick pressure release option and remove the lid as soon as the pressure has normalized.
4. Serve warm.

PORK CHOPS AND CABBAGE

This recipe needs 10 minutes of preparation, 15 minutes of cooking time and will serve 2.

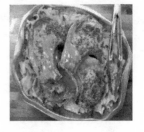

Nutrition Facts

Protein: 31 grams, Carbs: 35 grams
Fiber: 26 grams, Sugar: 11.2 grams
Fats: 18.2 grams, Calories: 412

Ingredients

- Pork chops (2)
- Fennel seeds (.5 tsp.)
- Black pepper (as desired)
- Cabbage (1 small head)
- Coconut oil (1.5 tsp.)
- Beef stock (.3 c)
- Almond flour (1 tsp.)

Preparation

1. Preheat cooker on sauté.
2. Sprinkle the chops with pepper, fennel, and salt.
3. Slice the cabbage into ¾ inch slices, set aside.
4. In preheated cooker, add oil and brown the chops on one side.
5. Remove the chops and add the cabbage.
6. Place the chops browned side up on the cabbage. Pour in the stock.
7. Cover and seal with lid.
8. Cook 8 minutes on high pressure.
9. Once finished, release the pressure. Remove the meat and cabbage and tent with foil.

10. Allow the juices to boil. Stir in the flour. Pour the sauce over the meat and cabbage and serve. Once the timer goes off, select the natural pressure release option and remove the lid as soon as the pressure has normalized.

11. Serve warm.

ROOT BEER PORK

This recipe needs 15 minutes of preparation, 35 minutes of cooking time and will serve 2.

Nutrition Facts

Protein: 19.7grams, Carbs: 26.2 grams
Fiber: 21.5 grams, Sugar: 0 grams
Fats: 17.2 grams, Calories: 323

Ingredients

- Pork roast (1 lb.)
- Black pepper (as desired)
- Onion (.6 c sliced)
- Root beet (.3 c)
- Ketchup (2 T)
- Almond flour (1.5 tsp)
- Lemon juice (.25 tsp)
- Worcestershire sauce (1.5 tsp)
- Tomato paste (1 T)
- Honey (1.5 tsp)

Preparation

1. Season roast with pepper and garlic salt, and put in the pot.
2. Mix the rest of the ingredients together and pour on the roast.
3. Lock and seal the lid.
4. Set to meat/stew for 35 minutes. Carefully release pressure
5. Take out onions and roast.
6. Discard the onions and shred the pork.
7. Stir the pork back into the pot.

MAPLE GLAZED PORK

This recipe needs 10 minutes of preparation, 15 minutes of cooking time and will serve 2.

Nutrition Facts

Protein: 23.8 grams, Carbs: 37.5 grams
Fiber: 32.8 grams, Sugar: 18.2 grams
Fats: 42 grams, Calories: 540

Ingredients

- Maple syrup (.25 c)
- Honey (.25 c)
- Cinnamon (1 tsp)
- Brown sugar (.25 c)
- Orange juice (2 T)
- Nutmeg (1 tsp)
- Bone in ham (1 small)

Preparation

1. Combine everything except for the ham in a saucepan on medium heat; mix well.
2. Put the ham in the cooker. Cook 15 minutes, then use quick release.
3. Set the ham in the baking dish. Pour glaze over ham.
4. Place the ham under a broiler to caramelize the sugars and form a slight char.

Chapter 5
Sea Food Meals

SEAFOOD PAELLA

This recipe needs 10 minutes of preparation, 10 minutes of cooking time and will serve 2.

Nutrition Facts

Protein: 30 grams, Carbs: 22.9 grams
Fiber: 16 grams, Sugar: 17 grams
Fats: 28 grams, Calories: 453

Ingredients – Fish stock

- Water (6 c)
- Parsley (1 bunch)
- Bay leaf (1)
- Celery (1 stalk)
- Carrots (2)
- Fish heads (4)

Ingredients - Paella

- Shirataki rice (1 c)
- Shellfish (1 c mixed)
- Seafood (.5 c)
- Turmeric (1 pinch)
- Low-sodium vegetable stock (1 c)
- Green bell pepper (.5 diced)
- Red bell pepper (.5 diced)
- Ghee (2 T)
- Onion (.5 diced)

Preparation

1. To make the fish stock, add all of the ingredients to the Instant Pot cooker before sealing it and selecting the high

pressure setting for 5 minutes. All the pressure to naturally release when the timer goes off. Set the stock aside.

2. To make the paella, start by setting the Instant Pot to sauté before adding in the ghee and allowing it to heat up fully before adding in the onion and peppers and allowing them to cook for about 3 minutes or until the onion begins to brown and soften.

3. Add in the rice and the seafood and let everything cook approximately 2 minutes. Reintroduce the fish stock along with the turmeric and mix well. Place shellfish on top (if applicable) but do not mix.

4. Seal the lid of the cooker, choose the high pressure and set the time for 6 minutes.

5. Once the timer goes off, select the natural pressure release option and remove the lid as soon as the pressure has normalized.

6. Mix well prior to serving.

INSTANT POT MAHI-MAHI

This recipe needs 10 minutes of preparation, 5 minutes of cooking time and will serve 2.

Nutrition Facts

Protein: 30 grams, Carbs: 19.5 grams
Fiber: 14.2 grams, Sugar: 3.5 grams
Fats: 12 grams, Calories: 253

Ingredients

- Orange juice (.5 T)
- Hot sauce (1 T)
- Nanami Togarashi (.5 T)
- Honey (1 T)
- Lime (.25 juiced)
- Ginger (.5 in grated)
- Garlic (1 clove minced)
- Black pepper (to taste)
- Mahi-mahi (2, 6 Oz filets)

Preparation

1. Season the fish as desired before setting it aside.
2. In a small mixing bowl, combine the orange juice, Nanami Togarashi, siracha, lime juice, honey, garlic and ginger together and mix well to form a spicy and sweet sauce.
3. Add 1 c water to the Instant Pot before adding in the steam rack and placing the filets on the rack in a single layer. Top the filets with sauce and ensure they are coated thoroughly.
4. Seal the lid of the cooker, choose the manual pressure option and set the time for 5 minutes.

5. Once the timer goes off, select the instant pressure release option and remove the lid as soon as the pressure has normalized.

6. Serve warm.

INSTANT POT COD

This recipe needs 10 minutes of preparation, 5 minutes of cooking time and will serve 2.

Nutrition Facts

Protein: 18 grams, Carbs: 7 grams
Fiber: 5 grams, Sugar: 4.8 grams
Fats: 23.4 grams, Calories: 263

Ingredients

- Earth balance butter (1 T)
- Pepper (as desired)
- Cherry tomatoes (.5 c)
- Cod (2, 6 oz. filets)
- Olive oil (1 T)

Preparation

1. Place a small, oven safe glass dish into your Instant Pot before placing your tomatoes inside of it. Place the code on top of the tomatoes in a single layer before seasoning as desired and drizzling with olive oil

2. Seal the lid of the cooker, choose the high-pressure option and set the time for 5 minutes.

3. Once the timer goes off, select the instant pressure release option and remove the lid as soon as the pressure has normalized.

4. Serve warm.

SPICY LEMON SALMON

This recipe needs 5 minutes of preparation, 5 minutes of cooking time and will serve 2.

Nutrition Facts

Protein: 17 grams, Carbs: 5.6 grams
Fiber: 3.9 grams, Sugar: .2 grams
Fats: 15.4 grams, Calories: 250

Ingredients

- Water (1 c)
- Pepper (as desired)
- Nanami Togarashi (1 T)
- Lemon (1 juiced, 1 sliced)
- Salmon (2, 6 oz. filets)

Preparation

1. Season the salmon using the pepper, Nanami and lemon juice.
2. Place the trivet into the bottom of the Instant Pot, taking care to ensure the handles remain up.
3. Add 1 c water to the Instant Pot cooker before placing the fish on the rack and topping with any remaining juice or seasoning.
4. Seal the lid of the cooker, choose the high-pressure option and set the time for 5 minutes.
5. Once the timer goes off, select the instant pressure release option and remove the lid as soon as the pressure has normalized to prevent the fish from over cooking.
6. Serve warm.

SHRIMP AND STEAMED ASPARAGUS

This recipe needs 10 minutes of preparation, 5 minutes of cooking time and will serve 2.

Nutrition Facts

Protein: 17 grams, Carbs: 5.6 grams
Fiber: 3.9 grams, Sugar: .2 grams
Fats: 15.4 grams, Calories: 250

Ingredients

- Cajun seasoning (.5 T)
- Olive oil (1 tsp)
- Asparagus (6 stalks)
- Shrimp (.5 lbs. deveined, peeled)

Preparation

1. Place the trivet into the bottom of the Instant Pot, taking care to ensure the handles remain up.
2. Add 1 c water to the Instant Pot cooker before placing the asparagus on the rack in a single layer before topping with the shrimp. Coat using the olive oil before seasoning using the Cajun seasoning.
3. Seal the lid of the cooker, choose the low-pressure option and set the time for 5 minutes.
4. Once the timer goes off, select the instant pressure release option and remove the lid as soon as the pressure has normalized to prevent the shrimp from over cooking.
5. Serve warm.

FRIED RICE WITH SHRIMP

This recipe needs 10 minutes of preparation, 10 minutes of cooking time and will serve 2.

Nutrition Facts

Protein: 20.4 grams, Carbs: 21 grams
Fiber: 38.5 grams, Sugar: 6.2 grams
Fats: 31.2 grams, Calories: 321
Sodium: 168 mg

Ingredients

- Water (1.5 c)
- Pepper (as desired)
- Ginger (.25 tsp ground)
- Cayenne pepper (.25 tsp)
- Carrots (.5 c sliced)
- Shrimp (deveined, peeled (4 oz.)
- Garlic (1 clove minced)
- Low-sodium soy sauce (.25 c)
- Onion (.5 c chopped)
- Sesame seed oil (2 T divided)
- Egg (1 beaten)
- Shirataki rice (1 c)

Preparation

1. Turn the Instant Pot cooker to sauté and allow it to heat fully. Add half of the sesame oil to the cooker and let it heat before adding in the eggs and scrambling them. When they are finished cooking, remove the eggs and set them aside.

2. Add the remaining oil to the Instant Pot cooker before adding in the onion and garlic and let them cook for about 5 minutes and the onion is brown and soft.

3. Turn off the heat before adding in the shrimp, carrots and rice. Season using the pepper, ginger and soy sauce and ensure everything is well coated. Add in water to ensure everything mixes well.

4. Seal the lid of the cooker, choose the rice option and leave the timer on the automatic setting.

5. Once the timer goes off, select the instant pressure release option and remove the lid as soon as the pressure has normalized to prevent the shrimp from over cooking.

6. Stir the results thoroughly and let them sit for an additional 5 minutes prior to serving.

7. Serve warm.

INSTANT POT CLAMS

This recipe needs 5 minutes of preparation, 5 minutes of cooking time and will serve 2.

Nutrition Facts

Protein: 17 grams, Carbs: 13.1 grams
Fiber: 8.5 grams, Sugar: 4.6 grams
Fats: 27.6 grams, Calories: 460

Ingredients

- Water (1 c)
- Pepper (as desired)
- Lemon (1 juiced)
- White wine (.25 c)
- Chicken broth (.25 c)
- Pale ale (1 c)
- Basil (.25 c)
- Garlic (1 c minced)
- Extra virgin olive oil (.25 c)

Preparation

1. Set the Instant Pot cooker to sauté before adding in the olive oil and allowing it to heat up fully. Add in the garlic and allow it to heat until it becomes fragrant. Mix in the water, lemon juice, wine, chicken broth and basil. Mix well and allow everything to boil for 60 seconds.

2. Place the trivet into the bottom of the Instant Pot, taking care to ensure the handles remain up. Place the steamer basket on to of it and place the clams inside of that.

3. Seal the lid of the cooker, choose the high-pressure option and set the time for 5 minutes.

4. Once the timer goes off, select the instant pressure release option and remove the lid as soon as the pressure has normalized to prevent the clams from over cooking. Discard those that did not open.

5. Remove the basket from the pot and place the clams in a serving bowel and top with the liquid from the Instant Pot.

6. Serve hot.

TIGER PRAWN RISOTTO

This recipe needs 30 minutes of preparation, 15 minutes of cooking time and will serve 2.

Nutrition Facts

Protein: 12 grams, Carbs: 22.1 grams
Fiber: 16.5 grams, Sugar:.2 grams
Fats: 28 grams, Calories: 221

Ingredients – Prawn Risotto

- Coconut oil (2T)
- Shirataki rice (.75 c)
- Spring onion (1 sprig sliced)
- Parmesan cheese (.25 c grated)
- Baking soda (.125 tsp)
- Tiger prawns (.25 lbs. unpeeled, frozen)
- Low-sodium miso paste (1 T)
- Low sodium soy sauce (1 T)
- Homemade fish stock (2 c)
- Cooking sake (.25 c)
- Shirataki rice (.5 c)
- Shallot (.5 minced)
- Garlic (1 clove minced)
- Unsalted butter (2 T)

Ingredients – Fish Stock

Preparation

1. To make the fish stock, add all of the ingredients to the Instant Pot cooker before sealing it and selecting the high pressure setting for 5 minutes. All the pressure to naturally release when the timer goes off. Set the stock aside.

2. Set the Instant Pot to sauté before adding in the olive oil and butter and allowing it to heat up fully before adding in the shallots and garlic and allowing them to cook for about 3 minutes.

3. Add in the prawns and allow them to cook until they are mostly done. Remove them from the Instant Pot cooker and set them aside.

4. Add in the rice and stir to coat evenly. Let it cook for two minutes before adding in the miso paste and soy sauce and mixing well. Add in the cooking sake to deglaze the pot. Let it boil for 60 seconds to ensure all the alcohol has evaporated.

5. Add in the fish stock before sealing the lid of the cooker, choose the high pressure and set the time for 5 minutes.

6. Peel the prawns while the risotto cooks

7. Once the timer goes off, select the instant pressure release option and remove the lid as soon as the pressure has normalized. If you prefer creamier risotto, then you will want to allow it to cook for an additional minute.

8. Toss in the onion and parmesan cheese and mix well prior to serving.

JAMBALAYA

This recipe needs 10 minutes of preparation, 10 minutes of cooking time and will serve 2.

Nutrition Facts

Protein: 21.1 grams, Carbs: 27.8 grams
Fiber: 20.9 grams, Sugar: 3.3 grams
Fats: 16.3 grams, Calories: 321

Ingredients

- Worcestershire sauce (.25 T)
- Creole seasoning (.25 T)
- Tomatoes (.5 c crushed)
- Chicken stock (1.75 c)
- Shirataki rice (.75 c)
- Garlic (2 T minced)
- Onion (2 c diced fine)
- Bell pepper (1 c diced)
- Prawns (.25 lbs.)
- Chicken (.25 lbs.)
- Olive oil (2 T)
- Shirataki rice (.75 c)

Preparation

1. Set the Instant Pot to sauté before coating the chicken using the creole seasoning and placing into the pot to brown completely. Once browned, remove it from the Instant Pot. Check the temperature with a meat thermometer, it should read close to 165 degrees F.

2. Add in the garlic, onion and peppers and allow everything to sauté for about 5 minutes or until the onion is soft and brown. Add in the rice and stir to coat.

3. Seal the lid of the cooker, choose the rice setting and leave the time at the default setting.

4. In a mixing bowl, combine the remaining ingredients with the chicken and mix well.

5. Once the timer goes off, select the instant pressure release option and remove the lid as soon as the pressure has normalized. Add in the remaining ingredients, reseal the lid, choose the high-pressure option and let everything cook an additional 2 minutes.

6. Serve warm.

Chapter 6
Vegetarian Meals

ARUGULA, BLOOD ORANGE AND SHIRATAKI SALAD

This recipe needs 5 minutes of preparation, 15 minutes of cooking time and will serve 2.

Nutrition Facts

Protein: 2.8 grams, Carbs: 7.7 grams
Fiber: 5.1 grams, Sugar: 0.04 grams
Fats: 8.6 grams, Calories: 126

Ingredients

- Earth balance butter (1 T)
- Shirataki rice (.75 c)
- Blood orange (.5 halved)
- Water (1 c)
- Cold pressed extra virgin olive oil (1 T)
- Lemon juice (.5 tsp)
- Romano cheese ribbons (3 T)
- Walnuts (3 T chopped rough)

Preparation

1. Add the shirataki rice to a bowl along with 1 c water and lemon juice and allow it to soak overnight. Drain prior to using.
2. Add the shirataki rice, along with the oil and 2 c water to the Instant Pot cooker pot, place the pot in the cooker and seal the lid.
3. Choose the high pressure setting and set the time for 15 minutes. When the Instant Pot cooker gets up to pressure you will then want to lower the temperature as much as possible while still maintaining pressure.

4. Once the timer goes off, select the natural pressure release option and remove the lid once the pressure has dropped completely.

5. Add all of the ingredients to a serving bowl and toss to combine.

ALMOND AND COCONUT RISOTTO

This recipe needs 20 minutes of preparation, 5 minutes of cooking time and will serve 2.

Nutrition Facts

Protein: 12 grams, Carbs: 14 grams
Fiber: 11 grams, Sugar: 11.2 grams
Fats: 27.1 grams, Calories: 88

Ingredients

- Agave syrup (2 T)
- Coconut flakes (2 T)
- Vanilla extract (1 tsp)
- Shirataki rice (.5 c)
- Coconut milk (.5 c)
- Almond milk (1 c)

Preparation

1. Set the Instant Pot to sauté before adding in almond and coconut milk, stirring constantly while it boils. Add in the rice and continue stirring to combine thoroughly.
2. Seal the lid of the cooker, choose the manual pressure setting and set the time for 5 minutes.
3. Once the timer goes off, select the natural pressure release option and wait until the remaining pressure has normalized.
4. Add in the agave syrup and vanilla extract and mix well.
5. Top with coconut flakes prior to serving.

BANANA BREAD

This recipe needs 20 minutes of preparation, 30 minutes of cooking time and will make one loaf.

Nutrition Facts

Protein: 22 grams, Carbs: 17.9 grams
Fiber: 14.7 grams, Sugar: 12.1 grams
Fats: 18.1 grams, Calories: 200

Ingredients

- Coconut milk (.3 c)
- Baking powder (1 tsp.)
- Bananas (1.5 mashed)
- Cream of tartar (1.5 tsp.)
- Vanilla (1 tsp.)
- Coconut sugar (75 c)
- Coconut oil (.3 c)
- Egg (1)
- Almond flour (1.5 c)

Preparation

1. In a bowl, make buttermilk by combining cream of tartar together with coconut milk. Set aside.
2. Cream together sugar and butter and add in egg together with vanilla extract. Stir well.
3. Add mashed bananas and stir well to combine
4. In a separate bowl, mix cassava flour, baking soda, baking powder and salt.
5. Gradually pour dry ingredients and blend wet ingredients and mix well to combine
6. Add in buttermilk mixture and cover with foil.

7. Using a seven-inch cake pan, pour in the mixture

8. In the Instant Cooker pot, add in 2 cups of water and set the metal trivet rack at the bottom of the Instant Pot.

9. Lower your cake pan to the trivet, close the lid and seal the pot

10. Press Manual to 30 minutes cook time.

11. When the timer goes off, allow it to naturally release pressure, about 15 minutes.

12. Once the pressure is gone, remove the link and lift the trivet and pan.

13. Remove the foil and allow your cake to cool in the pan.

14. The bread will quickly come off the pan once it has completely cooled.

RED CURRY

This recipe needs 15 minutes of preparation, 15 minutes of cooking time and will serve 2.

Nutrition Facts

Protein: 12 grams, Carbs: 25.9 grams
Fiber: 21.2 grams, Sugar: .7 grams
Fats: 22 grams, Calories: 350
Sodium: 197 mg

Ingredients

- Spinach (.3 c chopped)
- Cayenne powder (.5 tsp.)
- Paprika (.25 tsp.)
- Curry powder (1 T)
- Water (2 c)
- Vegetable bouillon (1 tsp.)
- Ginger (.25 T minced rough)
- Onion (.25 diced)
- Tomato paste (1 T0
- Shirataki noodles (.75 c)
- Coconut milk (.5 c)
- Coconut oil (2 T)

Preparation

1. Set the Instant Pot to sauté before adding in the coconut oil and allowing it to heat up fully before adding in the onion and garlic and allowing them to cook for about 4 minutes or until the onion begins to brown and soften.

2. Add all of the remaining ingredients, save the spinach, and stir regularly until the curry is finished cooking. You will know this is the case when you watch the oil break the surface.

3. Seal the lid of the cooker, choose the manual pressure setting and set the time for 15 minutes.

4. Once the timer goes off, select the natural pressure release option and wait until the remaining pressure has normalized which should take about 10 minutes.

5. Remove the lid, add in the spinach and allow it to wilt.

6. Serve warm.

VEGGIE PASTA

This recipe needs 10 minutes of preparation, 8 minutes of cooking time and will serve 2.

Nutrition Facts

Protein: 28 grams, Carbs: 32.1 grams
Fiber: 29 grams, Sugar: 3.2 grams
Fats: 25 grams, Calories:139

Ingredients

- Shirataki pasta (2 c)
- Carrots (.25 c julienned)
- Broccoli (.25 c florets)
- Baby spinach (.25 c)
- Lemon (1 slice)
- Red pepper flakes (.25 tsp.)
- Pepper (.25 tsp.)
- Miso (.25 tsp.)
- Vegetable broth (.5 c)

Preparation

1. Set the Instant Pot to sauté before adding in the pasta, seasonings and vegetables, save the spinach, and combine thoroughly.
2. Seal the lid of the cooker, choose the option for manual pressure and set the time for 8 minutes.
3. Once the timer goes off, select the natural pressure release option and remove the lid once the pressure has normalized.
4. Remove the lid and add in the spinach, leaving it time to wilt.
5. Serve warm.

ALMOND MEAL POLENTA

This recipe needs 15 minutes of preparation, 5 minutes of cooking time and will serve 2.

Nutrition Facts

Protein: 20.6 grams, Carbs: 9.3 grams
Fiber: 7.2 grams, Sugar: 2.7 grams
Fats: 7.5 grams, Calories: 189
Sodium: 164 mg

Ingredients

- Italian seasoning (1 tsp.)
- Almond meal polenta (.5 c)
- Vegetable broth (1.5 c)
- Herb mixture (2 T chopped rough)

Preparation

1. Add the broth to the Instant Pot cooker pot before seasoning with the Italian seasoning, whisk well before adding the polenta.
2. Seal the lid of the cooker, choose the porridge option and set the time for 5 minutes.
3. Once the timer goes off, select the natural pressure release option and remove the lid after 10 minutes the pressure has normalized.
4. Top with herbs and cheese prior to serving.

STUFFED PEPPER SOUP

This recipe needs 5 minutes of preparation, 25 minutes of cooking time and will serve 2.

Nutrition Facts

Protein: 68.7 grams, Carbs: 52.3 grams
Fiber: 46 grams, Sugar: 5.9 grams
Fats: 20 grams, Calories: 134

Ingredients

- Cornmeal (1.5 T)
- Shirataki rice (1 c)
- Vegetable broth (.25 c)
- Tomatoes (7 oz. diced)
- Bell pepper (1)
- Black pepper (.5 tsp.)
- Chili powder (.5 tsp.)
- Cumin (.5 tsp.)
- Tomato paste (.25 can)
- Onion (.25 sliced thin)
- Olive oil (.5 T)

Preparation

1. Set the Instant Pot to sauté before adding in the olive oil and allowing it to heat up fully before adding in the onion and garlic and allowing them to cook for about 3 minutes or until the onion begins to brown and soften.

2. Turn off the sauté option before stirring in the tomato paste along with the black pepper and cumin along with the diced tomatoes, pepper and vegetable broth. Finally, add in the rice and mix until everything is blended.

3. Seal the lid of the cooker, choose the high pressure and set the time for 25 minutes.

4. Once the timer goes off, select the instant pressure release option and remove the lid as soon as the pressure has normalized.

5. Add in the cornmeal and stir well to prevent clumping.

6. Serve warm.

Chapter 7
Vegan Meals

UNSALTED BUTTERNUT SQUASH AND SHIRATAKI RICE RISOTTO

This recipe needs 10 minutes of preparation, 20 minutes of cooking time and will serve 2.

Nutrition Facts

Protein: 11.7 grams, Carbs: 23.5 grams
Fiber: 22 grams, Sugar: .5 grams
Fats: 12 grams, Calories: 410

Ingredients

- Pepper (as desired)
- Unsalted butternut squash (.5 c)
- Shirataki rice (1 c)
- Vegetable broth (1.75 c divided)
- Yellow onion (.25 c)
- Olive oil (2 T)
- Yeast (.75 T)
- Chard (1.5 c)
- Spinach (1.5 c)
- Red pepper (as desired)
- Garlic (1.5 cloves minced)
- Oregano (.25 tsp.)
- White wine (.25 c)
- Coriander (.5 tsp)

Preparation

1. Add the olive oil to Instant Pot cooker pot before turning the Instant Pot cooker to sauté. Add in the squash, garlic and onions and allow them to sauté for 5 minutes until the onions are soft and brown.

2. Add in the shirataki rice before combining thoroughly and then adding in the pepper, wine and vegetable broth and stirring well.

3. Seal the lid on the Instant Pot cooker and choose the manual option and set the time for 5 minutes.

4. Once the timer goes off, select the instant pressure release option and stir in the yeast along with the greens and let everything thicken 5 minutes prior to serving.

GREEN BEAN CASSEROLE

This recipe needs 5 minutes of preparation, 15 minutes of cooking time and will serve 2.

Nutrition Facts

Protein: 19.7 grams, Carbs: 11 grams
Fiber: 5.9 grams, Sugar: 9.7 grams
Fats: 35.1 grams, Calories: 757

Ingredients

- Green beans (4 oz.)
- Coconut oil (2 T)
- Onion (.5)
- Mushrooms (3 sliced)
- Coconut milk (.25 c)
- Vegetable broth (.5 c)

Preparation

1. Turn the Instant Pot cooker to sauté. After it warms up, add in the coconut oil before adding in the mushrooms and onion and allowing them to cook for 3 minutes.

2. Add the remaining ingredients into the Instant Pot cooker and seal the lid. Choose the high-pressure option and set the time for 15 minutes.

3. Once the timer goes off, select the instant pressure release option and add in 1 T cornstarch to allow everything to thicken.

4. Let sit five minutes prior to serving.

REFRIED BEANS

This recipe needs 20 minutes of preparation, 20 minutes of cooking time and will serve 2.

Nutrition Facts

Protein: 29.2 grams, Carbs: 15.2 grams
Fiber: 12.8 grams, Sugar: 5.2 grams
Fats: 37.5 grams, Calories: 541

Ingredients

- Black pepper (as desired)
- Green chilies (4 oz. diced)
- Garlic (1 T minced)
- Yellow onion (.25 c chopped)
- Olive oil (1.5 T)
- Low-sodium pinto beans (.5 c)

Preparation

1. In Instant Pot, add in beans at the bottom and cover with enough water, about 2 inches.
2. Add 1 tablespoon olive oil and then lock lid and cook on high pressure for 20 minutes.
3. When timer goes off, let the pressure release on its own
4. Add chopped onions, minced garlic, canned chilies and salt
5. Lock lid again and pressure cook on high for 10 minutes.
6. Release pressure naturally. Remove lid and mash beans to desired consistency. Do not liquefy. Remove beans from pot.
7. Clean pot and turn to sauté, add beans again and simmer on low heat, stirring often until beans have thickened to desired consistency. About 10 minutes.

VEGETABLE RISOTTO

This recipe needs 10 minutes of preparation, 5 minutes of cooking time and will serve 2.

Nutrition Facts

Protein: 12 grams, Carbs: 34.9 grams
Fiber: 33.7 grams, Sugar: 22.2 grams
Fats: 7.5 grams, Calories: 214
Sodium: 80 mg

Ingredients

- Earth balance butter (1 T)
- Tomato (.25 diced)
- Shirataki rice (.75 c)
- Acorn squash (.25 c)
- Onion (.25 c minced)
- Eggplant (.25 c diced)
- Nutritional yeast (.25 T)
- Pepper (to taste)
- Zucchini (.25 c)
- Olive oil (1 tsp)
- Garlic (.5 cloves)
- White wine (2 T)
- Vegetable broth (1 c)

Preparation

1. Set the Instant Pot to sauté before adding in the olive oil and allowing it to heat up fully before adding in the onion and garlic and allowing them to cook for about 3 minutes or until the onion begins to brown and soften.

2. Mix in the vegetables and stir for about 15 minutes until they soften. Mix in the shirataki rice and coat thoroughly.

3. Add in the oregano, wine, pepper and broth, mix well and seal the lid of the cooker. Choose the manual option and set the time for 5 minutes.

4. Once the timer goes off, select the instant pressure release option and remove the lid as soon as possible to ensure it doesn't overcook.

5. Mix the nutritional yeast along with the earth balance butter before letting everything sit and thicken for approximately 5 minutes.

6. Serve warm.

CURRIED SPINACH

This recipe needs 5 minutes of preparation, 5 minutes of cooking time and will serve 2.

Nutrition Facts

Protein: 12 grams, Carbs: 22.9 grams, Fiber: 19 grams, Sugar: 11.2 grams, Fats: 28 grams, Calories: 453

Ingredients

- Cumin (.25 tsp)
- Coriander (.25 tsp.)
- Cayenne pepper (.25 tsp)
- Black pepper (.5 tsp.)
- Garam masala (.25 tsp.)
- Garlic (1 clove minced)
- Ginger (.25 in minced)
- Onion (.25 diced)
- Earth balance butter (.5 T)
- Spinach (.75 lbs. rinsed)

Preparation

1. Set the Instant Pot to sauté before adding in the earth balance butter and allowing it to heat up fully before adding in the onion, ginger and garlic and allowing them to cook for about 3 minutes or until the onion begins to brown and soften. Add in the spinach and allow it to sauté until it starts to wilt.

2. Select the keep warm option and seal the lid of the cooker before switching to the poultry setting and allowing

everything to cook on a high pressure for approximately 15 minutes.

3. Once the timer goes off, select the natural pressure release option and allow the mixture to cool for 10 minutes before carefully removing the lid and transferring the contents to a blender.

4. Blend as desired before adding back to the Instant Pot to keep warm while serving.

Conclusion

Thank you for making it through to the end of Instant Pot Cookbook for Two let's hope it was informative and able to provide you with all of the tools you need to achieve your goals, whatever it is that they may be. Just because you've finished this book doesn't mean there is nothing left to learn on the topic, expanding your horizons is the only way to find the mastery you seek.

Remember, this book isn't designed to be the end all and be all when it comes to Instant Pot recipes, instead it should be thought of more as a blueprint for the possibilities that are available thanks to the Instant Pot cooker. The Instant Pot cooker provides users with the opportunity to cook a much wider variety of foods than their circumstances or surroundings may otherwise allow for. Take advantage of the new opportunities it provides to you and expand your culinary horizons; you never know when your new favorite food may be just around the corner.

Finally, if you found this book useful in any way, a review on Amazon is always appreciated!